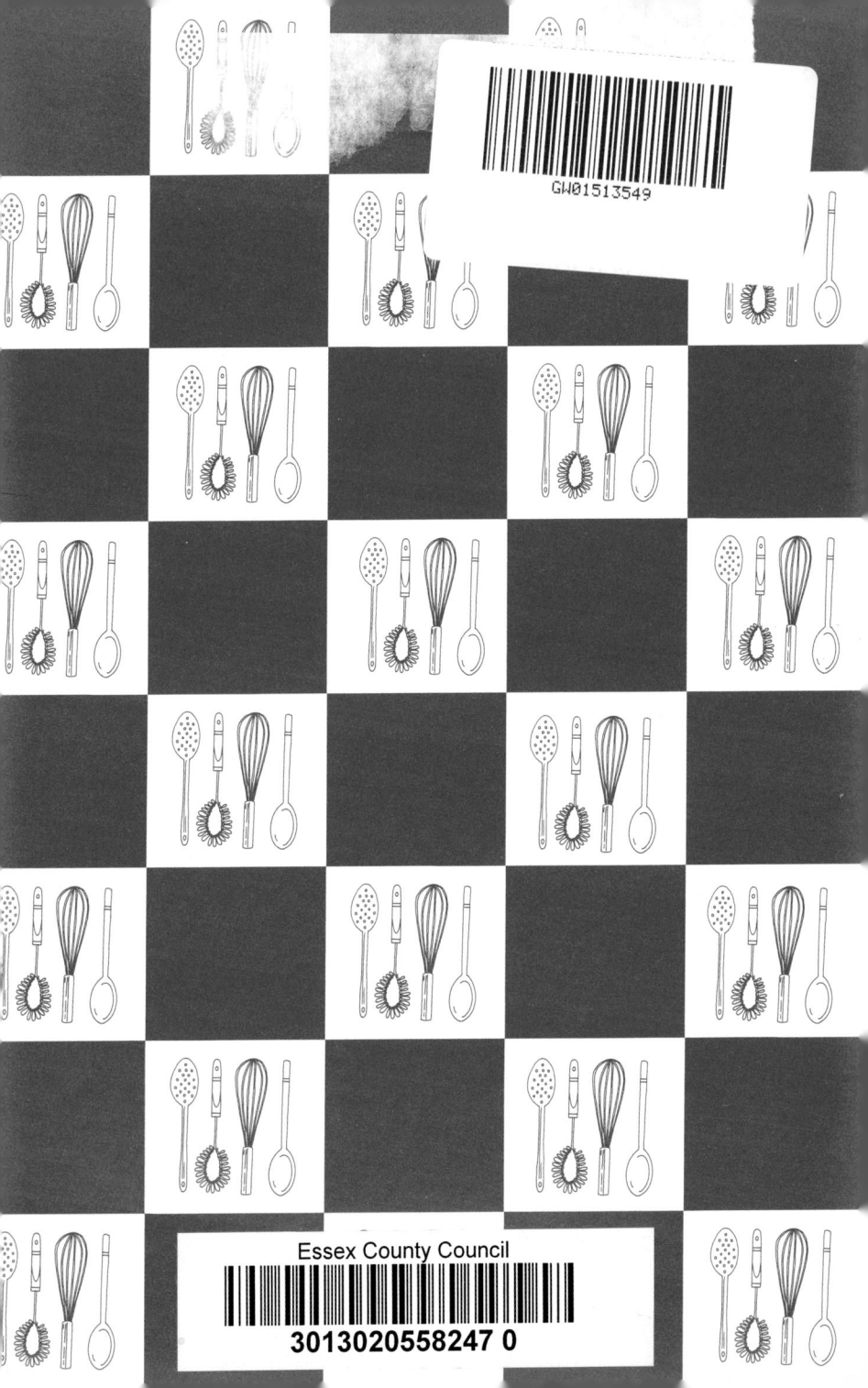

COOKING FOR CHRISTMAS

Valerie Ferguson

LORENZ BOOKS

Contents

Introduction   4

Countdown to Christmas   6

Techniques   7

Basic Recipes   9

Festive Soups & Starters   10

Main Courses   22

Vegetables & Stuffings   42

Desserts, Puddings & Baking   50

Index   64

Introduction

Christmas is a time for celebrations, a time for entertaining family and friends and sharing the best of festive food and good cheer with them. Cooking for Christmas can seem like entering a marathon, though, and not even the keenest cook wants to spend the festive season imprisoned in the kitchen. This book includes recipes that can be cooked ahead to make the festive period as stress-free and enjoyable as possible.

To make life easier for yourself over the busy Christmas holiday, try to prepare as much as you can in advance and finish off, or reheat, on the day. Planning is essential: draw up lists, give yourself ample time to shop and don't forget to allow time to pick up last-minute fresh foods. Make full use of your freezer, too – desserts, pastries and stuffings, for example, can all be made ahead and frozen.

On the big day, allow yourself plenty of time, stay calm and don't be afraid to draft in the rest of the family to help. All this should give you freedom to enjoy the company of family and friends to the full.

This practical little book features traditional roasts, elegant fish dishes and vegetarian alternatives, so that everyone can celebrate in style.

Introduction

Countdown to Christmas

This at-a-glance timetable will help you plan and organize your Christmas cooking for a traditional dinner with turkey.

Late autumn:
Make preserves and relishes to serve with cold meats over the festive season.

November:
Second week. Make Moist & Rich Christmas Cake.
Fourth week. Make Christmas Pudding. Decide on Christmas dinner menu. Order turkey, goose, beef or ham.

December:
First week. Make mincemeat. Compile complete shopping list for main Christmas meals under headings for different stores, or for the various counters at the supermarket. Continue to add to list throughout the week.
Second week. Shop for dry goods such as rice, dried fruits and flour. Order special bread requirements. Order milk, cream and other dairy produce. Make brandy butter.
Third week. Cover Moist & Rich Christmas Cake with fondant icing and decorate, leave 1 day, then cover and store.
Fourth week. Shop for chilled ingredients. Buy wines and other drinks.

21 December:
Check thawing time for frozen turkey, duck, beef or other meat. Large turkeys (11.5 kg/25 lb) need 86 hours (3½ days) to thaw in the fridge, or 40 hours at room temperature. Make a note to take the meat from the freezer at the appropriate time.

23 December:
Shop for fresh vegetables, if not possible to do so on 24 December.

24 December:
Shop for fresh vegetables, if possible. Assemble Christmas Salad and refrigerate dressing separately. Make stuffing for poultry.

Christmas Day:
This timetable is planned for Christmas dinner to be served at 2.00pm. If you wish to serve it at a different time, please adjust the times quoted accordingly.

Stuff poultry. Form leftover stuffing into balls or spoon into a greased ovenproof dish.
Set table, if not already done.
Put steamer or large pan on cooker and bring water to the boil at 10.40 am.
Put Christmas Pudding on to steam.

To cook a 5.5 kg/ 12 lb turkey
9.05am Preheat oven to 200°C/400°F/ Gas 6.
9.25am Put turkey in oven, covered.
9.45am Reduce heat to 180°C/350°F/ Gas 4. Baste turkey now and at frequent intervals.
12.15pm Put potatoes around meat. Remove foil from turkey and baste again. Turn the potatoes.
12.45pm Increase heat to 200°C/400°F/ Gas 6. Put any dishes of stuffing in oven.
1.45pm Remove turkey and potatoes from oven, put on heated dish, cover with foil and keep warm. Make gravy.
2.00pm Serve.

Techniques

Times for Roasting Turkey

When choosing a turkey for Christmas, you should allow about 450 g/1 lb of dressed (plucked and oven-ready) bird per head. A good estimate of the size of turkey to buy for Christmas is 4.5 kg/10 lb. This will serve about 12 people, with leftovers for the following day.

Oven-ready weight	Thawing time	Number of servings	Cooking time
3.5 kg/8 lb	18 hours	8–10 people	2½–3½ hours
4.5 kg/10 lb	19 hours	12–14 people	3½–4 hours
5.5 kg/12 lb	20 hours	16–18 people	3¾–4½ hours
6.3 kg/14 lb	24 hours	18–20 people	4–5 hours

These times apply to a turkey weighed after stuffing and at room temperature. Cook in a moderate oven, 180°C/350°F/Gas 4, covered with butter and bacon rashers and loosely covered with foil.

To test whether the turkey is fully cooked, push a skewer into the thickest part of the leg and press the flesh: the juices should run clear and free from any blood. If not, cook for a little longer and test again.

Carving a Turkey

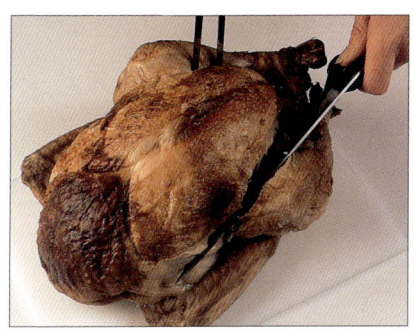

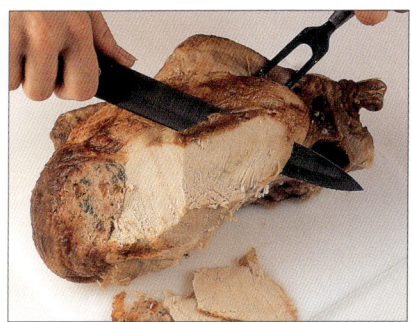

1 Remove the leg, cutting between the bones at the joint. Cut the leg in two through the joint and carve into slices. Remove the wing, cutting through the joint as for the leg.

2 Carve the breast in thin slices, starting at the front. Then carve slices from the back of the breast. Continue to carve, alternating the direction of carving in this way.

Cutting Vegetable Matchsticks

These decorative shapes, also called 'julienne', are simple to cut yet look very special. Matchsticks can be steamed, stir-fried, added to soups, used as a garnish or to give an extra crunch to salads.

1 Peel the vegetable and shave off curved edges. Cut across into pieces about 5 cm/2 in long.

2 Lay each piece flat and cut it lengthways into slices 3mm/⅛ in thick or less, guiding the side of the knife with your knuckles. Stack the vegetable slices and cut them lengthways into strips about 3mm/⅛ in thick or less.

Chopping Onions Finely

Many dishes use chopped onions as an essential flavouring. Stuffings, for example, require evenly chopped, small pieces.

1 Peel the onion. Cut it in half and set it down on a board. Make lengthways vertical cuts along it, cutting almost, but not quite through, to the root. Make two horizontal cuts from the stalk end towards the root, but not through it.

2 Cut the onion crossways to form small, even dice. This can be done in advance and kept in a covered bowl in the refrigerator until required.

Basic Recipes

Cranberry Sauce
This is the sauce for roast turkey and any white roast meat.

Serves 6

INGREDIENTS
1 orange
225 g/8 oz/2 cups cranberries
225 g/8 oz/generous 1 cup sugar

1 Pare the rind thinly from the orange, taking care not to remove any white pith. Squeeze the juice.

2 Place the rind and juice in a saucepan with the cranberries, sugar and 150 ml/¼ pint/⅔ cup water.

3 Bring to the boil, stirring, then simmer for 15 minutes or until the berries burst. Remove the rind and cool the sauce before serving.

Fondant Icing
This icing can be used for modelling decorations as well as covering a cake.

Makes enough to cover a 20 cm/8 in round cake

INGREDIENTS
15 g/½ oz/1 tbsp powdered gelatine
60 ml/4 tbsp water
10 ml/2 tsp liquid glucose
500 g/1¼ lb/5 cups
 icing (confectioners')sugar

1 Sprinkle the gelatine over the water in a bowl and soak for 2 minutes. Place the bowl in a pan of hot water and dissolve over very gentle heat. Remove and add the glucose.

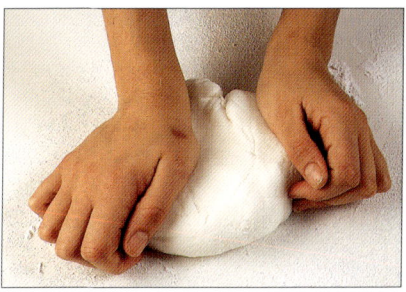

2 Sift the icing sugar into a bowl and add the gelatine mixture. Combine and then knead to a smooth paste.

Royal Icing
This icing will dry very hard.

Makes enough to cover a 20 cm/8 in round cake

INGREDIENTS
2 egg whites
5 ml/1 tsp lemon juice
5 ml/1 tsp glycerine (optional)
450 g/1 lb/4 cups icing (confectioners') sugar

1 In a large bowl, beat together the egg whites, lemon juice and glycerine (if using) with a fork. Gradually sift in enough icing sugar to make a thick paste. Using a wooden spoon, stir in the remaining icing sugar until the icing forms stiff peaks.

Pear & Watercress Soup

A new twist on a traditional combination of flavours.

Serves 6

INGREDIENTS
1 bunch watercress
4 medium pears, sliced
900 ml/1½ pints/3¾ cups chicken stock, preferably home-made
120 ml/4 fl oz/½ cup double (heavy) cream
juice of 1 lime
salt and freshly ground black pepper

FOR THE CROUTONS
25 g/1 oz/2 tbsp butter
15 ml/1 tbsp olive oil
200 g/7 oz/3 cups cubed stale bread
115 g/4 oz/1 cup chopped Stilton cheese

1 Reserve a third of the watercress leaves. Place the remainder in a pan with the pears, stock and a little seasoning. Simmer for 15–20 minutes. Place in a food processor or blender with most of the reserved watercress and blend until smooth.

2 Transfer to a clean pan and add the cream and lime juice. Season again to taste. Reheat gently until the soup is warmed through.

3 To make the croûtons, melt the butter and oil and fry the bread cubes until golden brown. Drain. Put the cheese on top and grill until bubbling. Serve the soup with the croûtons and remaining watercress.

Broccoli & Almond Soup

Serves 4–6

INGREDIENTS
50 g/2 oz/½ cup ground almonds
675 g/1½ lb broccoli, divided into
  small florets
900 ml/1½ pints/3¾ cups vegetable
  stock or water
300 ml/½ pint/1¼ cups skimmed milk
salt and freshly ground black pepper

1 Preheat the oven to 180°C/350°F/Gas 4. Spread the ground almonds evenly on a baking sheet and toast in the oven for about 10 minutes or until they are golden brown.

2 Reserve a quarter of the toasted almonds and set aside for the garnish. Steam the broccoli for 6–7 minutes or until tender.

3 Place the remaining toasted almonds, the broccoli, stock or water and milk in a blender and blend until smooth. Season to taste.

4 Reheat the soup, pour into warmed bowls and serve sprinkled with the reserved toasted almonds.

Christmas Salad

Prepare this light first course ahead and assemble just before serving.

Serves 8

INGREDIENTS
mixed red and green lettuce leaves
2 sweet pink grapefruit
1 large or 2 small avocados, peeled, stoned and cubed

FOR THE DRESSING
90 ml/6 tbsp light olive oil
30 ml/2 tbsp red wine vinegar
1 garlic clove, crushed
5 ml/1 tsp Dijon mustard
salt and freshly ground black pepper

FOR THE CARAMELIZED ORANGE PEEL
4 oranges
50 g/2 oz/¼ cup caster (superfine) sugar
60 ml/4 tbsp cold water

2 Put the sugar and water in a small pan and heat gently until the sugar has dissolved. Then add the shreds of orange rind and boil for 5 minutes until the rind is tender. Using two forks, remove the orange rind from the syrup and spread it out on a wire rack to dry. (This can be done the day before.) Reserve the syrup to add to the dressing.

1 To make the caramelized peel, using a vegetable peeler, remove the rind from the oranges in thin strips and reserve the fruit. Scrape away the white pith from the underside of the rind with a sharp knife, and then cut the rind into fine shreds.

3 Tear the lettuce into bite-size pieces. Peel the grapefruit and remove the pith from them and the oranges. Holding the fruit over a bowl to catch any juice, cut them into segments, removing all the pith.

FESTIVE SOUPS & STARTERS

4 Put all the dressing ingredients into a screw-top jar and shake vigorously. Add the reserved orange-flavoured syrup and adjust the seasoning to taste. Arrange all the salad ingredients on individual plates, spoon over the dressing and scatter on the caramelized orange peel.

Layered Salmon Terrine

This elegant fish mousse is perfect for a buffet or first course.

Serves 8

INGREDIENTS
200 ml/7 fl oz/scant 1 cup milk
50 g/2 oz/4 tbsp butter
65 g/2½ oz/9 tbsp plain (all-purpose) flour
450 g/1 lb each of fresh haddock and salmon fillet, boned and skinned
2 eggs, separately beaten
60 ml/4 tbsp double (heavy) cream
115 g/4 oz smoked salmon or trout, cut into strips
salt and freshly ground black pepper
lemon slices and sprigs of fresh parsley, to garnish

1 Heat the milk and butter in a pan until the milk is boiling. Draw the pan aside and beat in the flour until a thick, smooth paste forms. Season, turn out on to a plate and leave to cool.

2 Process the haddock in a food processor until smooth. Put it into a bowl. Process the salmon in the same way and put into a separate bowl.

3 Add an egg and half the cream to each bowl. Beat half the milk and flour paste into each mixture.

4 Preheat the oven to 180°C/350°F/Gas 4. Butter a 900 g/2 lb loaf tin and line with greaseproof paper. Lay strips of smoked salmon or trout diagonally over the base and up the sides.

5 Spoon the haddock mixture into the tin and level the surface. Cover with the salmon mixture and fold over the smoked fish strips.

6 Cover the tin with buttered greaseproof (waxed) paper and then foil. Place in a roasting tin and pour round enough hot water to come halfway up the sides of the tin. Cook the terrine for 40 minutes or until firm.

7 Remove from the oven and stand for 10 minutes. Turn the terrine out on to a serving plate and serve warm or cold with the garnishes.

Roquefort & Cucumber Mousse

The robust flavour of blue cheese is partnered with cool cucumber in this creamy starter dish which is easily prepared ahead of time.

Serves 6

INGREDIENTS
10 ml/2 tsp powdered gelatine
75 ml/5 tbsp cold water
90 g/3½ oz Roquefort cheese
200 g/7 oz/scant 1 cup full-, medium- or low-fat soft (farmer's) cheese
45 ml/3 tbsp crème fraîche or soured cream
18 cm/7 in piece cucumber, peeled, quartered lengthways and cut into 2.5 cm/1 in pieces
cayenne or white pepper
seedless red and green grapes and mint leaves, to garnish

1 Sprinkle the powdered gelatine over the cold water in a small heatproof bowl. Leave to soften for about 2 minutes, then place the bowl in a shallow pan of simmering water. Heat the mixture until the gelatine is dissolved, stirring occasionally.

2 In a food processor, process the cheeses and the crème fraîche or soured cream until smooth. Add the dissolved gelatine and process to blend. Add the pieces of cucumber and pulse to chop finely without completely reducing it to a purée. Season with cayenne or white pepper.

3 Rinse a 1.5 litre/2½ pint/6¼ cup dish or mould with cold water. Spoon in the mixture and tap gently to remove any air bubbles. Chill for 4–6 hours or overnight until well set.

4 To turn out, run a knife around the edge of the dish or mould and dip in hot water for 10–15 seconds. Place a large plate over the top of the dish and invert both together, shaking firmly to release the mousse. Garnish with grapes and mint leaves.

Chicken Liver Pâté

Served with onion marmalade, this is an elegant yet easy first course.

Serves 6–8

INGREDIENTS
1 small onion, finely chopped
175 g/6 oz/¾ cup butter, diced
1 garlic clove, finely chopped
450 g/1 lb chicken livers, trimmed
2.5 ml/½ tsp dried thyme
30–45 ml/2–3 tbsp brandy
salt and freshly ground black pepper
green salad, to serve

FOR THE ONION MARMALADE
25 g/1 oz/2 tbsp butter
450 g/1 lb red onions, thinly sliced
1 garlic clove, finely chopped
2.5 ml/½ tsp dried thyme
30–45 ml/2–3 tbsp raspberry or red wine vinegar
15–30 ml/1–2 tbsp clear honey
40 g/1½ oz/¼ cup sultanas (golden raisins)

1 Fry the onion in 25 g/1 oz/2 tbsp of the butter for 5–7 minutes until golden, then add the garlic and cook for 1 minute more. Add the chicken livers, thyme, salt and pepper. Cook for 3–5 minutes until the livers are coloured. Add the brandy and cook for a further minute.

2 Transfer to a food processor and process for 1 minute or until smooth. With the machine running, add the remaining butter, a few pieces at a time, until it is incorporated.

3 Press the mousse mixture through a fine sieve with a wooden spoon or rubber spatula. Use clear film (plastic wrap) line a 450 g/1 lb loaf tin. Pour in the mousse mixture and smooth the top. Cool, cover and chill until firm.

4 To make the onion marmalade, fry the onions gently in the butter for 20 minutes until softened and just coloured. Add the remaining ingredients and cook, covered, for 10–15 minutes until the onions are jam-like. Spoon into a bowl and cool.

FESTIVE SOUPS & STARTERS

5 To serve the pâté, dip the tin into hot water for 5 seconds and invert on to a board. Lift off the tin, peel off the clear film and smooth the surface of the pâté with a knife. Cut into slices and serve with a little of the onion marmalade and a green salad.

COOK'S TIP: The mousse will keep for 3–4 days if covered and chilled. The marmalade can be made up to 2 days ahead and reheated over a low heat or in the microwave until just warm.

Stilton Tartlets

These can be made in shallow tartlet tins to serve hot as a first course. You could also make them in tiny cocktail tins and serve as warm canapés.

Makes 12

INGREDIENTS
175 g/6 oz/1½ cups plain (all-purpose) flour
115 g/4 oz/½ cup butter
1 egg yolk
30 ml/2 tbsp cold water

FOR THE FILLING
15 g/½ oz/1 tbsp butter
15 g/½ oz/2 tbsp plain (all-purpose) flour
150 ml/¼ pint/⅔ cup milk
115 g/4 oz/1 cup Stilton
   cheese, crumbled
150 ml/¼ pint/⅔ cup double (heavy) cream
2.5 ml/½ tsp dried mixed herbs
3 egg yolks
salt and freshly ground black pepper

1 Sift the flour and a pinch of salt into a bowl and rub in the butter to make breadcrumbs. Mix the egg yolk with the water and stir in to make a soft dough. Knead until smooth, wrap in clear film (plastic wrap) and chill for 30 minutes.

2 To make the filling, melt the butter, stir in the flour and then the milk. Boil to thicken, stirring. Off the heat, beat in the cheese and season. Cool. Bring the cream and herbs to the boil. Reduce to 30 ml/2 tbsp. Beat into the sauce with the egg yolks.

3 Preheat the oven to 190°C/375°F/Gas 5. On a floured work surface, roll out the pastry 3 mm/⅛ in thick. Stamp out rounds with a fluted cutter and use to line your chosen tartlet tins.

4 Divide the filling among the tartlets: they should be filled only two-thirds full. Stamp out smaller fluted rounds or star shapes for the tops and lay on top of each tartlet. Bake for 20–25 minutes or until puffed and golden brown.

COOK'S TIP: The shortcrust pastry can also be made in a food processor, if you prefer.

MAIN COURSES

Roast Turkey

Serve with stuffing balls, roast potatoes, Brussels sprouts and gravy.

Serves 8

INGREDIENTS
4.5 kg/10 lb oven-ready turkey, with giblets (thawed if frozen)
1 large onion, peeled and stuck with 6 whole cloves
50 g/2 oz/4 tbsp butter, softened
10 chipolata sausages
salt and freshly ground black pepper
fresh herbs, to garnish

FOR THE STUFFING
225 g/8 oz rindless streaky bacon, chopped
1 large onion, finely chopped
450 g/1 lb pork sausagemeat
25 g/1 oz/⅓ cup rolled oats
30 ml/2 tbsp chopped fresh parsley
10 ml/2 tsp dried mixed herbs
1 large egg, beaten
115 g/4 oz/½ cup dried apricots, finely chopped

FOR THE GRAVY
25 g/1 oz/¼ cup plain (all-purpose) flour
450 ml/¾ pint/scant 2 cups giblet stock

1 Preheat the oven to 200°C/400°F/Gas 6. To make the stuffing, cook the bacon and onion until the bacon is crisp and the onion tender. Mix with the remaining ingredients and season well. Stuff the neck end of the turkey. Reserve any remaining stuffing.

2 Put the whole clove-studded onion inside the turkey. Weigh the bird and calculate the cooking time: allow 20 minutes per 450 g/1 lb plus 15 minutes over. Place the turkey in a large roasting tin.

3 Spread the turkey with the butter and season. Cover with foil and cook for 30 minutes. Baste with the pan juices. Lower the temperature to 180°C/350°F/Gas 4 and cook for the rest of the calculated time (allow about 3½ hours for a 4.5 kg/10 lb bird). Baste every 30 minutes.

4 Shape the remaining stuffing into small balls. Place on a baking tray and cook in the oven for 20 minutes or until golden brown.

5 About 20 minutes before the end of cooking put the sausages in the oven. Remove the foil from the turkey for the last hour of cooking.

MAIN COURSES

6 To test when the turkey is thoroughly cooked, insert a metal skewer into the thickest part of the thigh: the juices should run clear when the turkey is cooked. If the juices are still pink return the turkey to the oven and cook for another ten minutes before testing it again.

7 Transfer the turkey to a plate, cover with foil and leave to stand for about 15 minutes before carving. To make the gravy, spoon off the fat from the tin, leaving the meat juices. Blend in the flour and cook for 2 minutes. Add the stock, bring to the boil, season and pour into a sauce boat. To serve the turkey, surround with sausages and stuffing balls and garnish with herbs.

Roast Goose with Caramelized Apples

Choose a young goose with a pliable breast bone.

Serves 8

INGREDIENTS
4.5–5.5 kg/10–12 lb goose, with giblets
30 ml/2 tbsp plain (all-purpose) flour
600 ml/1 pint/2½ cups giblet stock
juice of 1 orange
salt and freshly ground black pepper

FOR THE STUFFING
225 g/8 oz/1 cup prunes, soaked overnight in 150 ml/¼ pint/⅔ cup port
675 g/1½ lb cooking apples, peeled, cored and cubed
1 large onion, chopped
4 celery sticks, sliced
15 ml/1 tbsp dried mixed herbs
finely grated rind of 1 orange
1 goose liver, chopped
450 g/1 lb pork sausagemeat
115 g/4 oz/1 cup chopped pecans or walnuts
2 eggs

FOR THE CARAMELIZED APPLES
50 g/2 oz/4 tbsp butter
60 ml/4 tbsp redcurrant jelly
30 ml/2 tbsp red wine vinegar
8 small dessert apples, peeled and cored

1 Stone (pit) and chop the prunes, reserving the port. Mix with the remaining stuffing ingredients and season. Add half the reserved port.

2 Preheat the oven to 200°C/400°F/Gas 6. Fill the neck end and cavity of the goose with the prepared stuffing. Weigh the bird and calculate the cooking time required: allow 15 minutes per 450 g/1 lb.

3 Put the bird on a rack in a roasting tin (pan) and rub the skin with salt. Prick the skin all over to help the fat run out. Roast the goose for 30 minutes, then reduce the heat to 180°C/350°F/Gas 4 and continue to roast for the remaining cooking time. Baste with a little cold water during cooking to crisp the skin.

4 To make the caramelized apples, melt the butter, redcurrant jelly and red wine vinegar in an ovenproof dish in the oven. Put in the prepared apples in a single layer and cook for 15–20 minutes, basting occasionally.

MAIN COURSES

5 Lift the goose on to a serving dish and let stand for 15 minutes before carving. Pour off the excess fat from the tin, leaving any sediment. Add the flour, cook until golden brown and add the stock. Bring to the boil.

6 Add the remaining reserved port, orange juice and seasoning. Simmer the gravy for 2–3 minutes. Strain into a gravy boat. Surround the goose with the caramelized apples and spoon over the redcurrant glaze.

Main Courses

Roast Pheasant with Port

This recipe is best for very young pheasants, particularly hen birds.

Serves 4

INGREDIENTS
2 oven-ready hen pheasants, about
    675 g/1½ lb each
sunflower oil, for brushing
50 g/2 oz/4 tbsp unsalted butter, softened
8 fresh thyme sprigs
2 bay leaves
6 streaky bacon rashers
15 ml/1 tbsp plain (all-purpose) flour
175 ml/6 fl oz/¾ cup game or chicken stock
15 ml/1 tbsp redcurrant jelly
45–60 ml/3–4 tbsp port
salt and freshly ground black pepper

1 Preheat the oven to 230°C/450°F/Gas 8. Line a roasting tin (pan) with a sheet of foil large enough to enclose the pheasants. Brush the foil with oil.

2 Carefully loosen the skin of the pheasants' breasts. Spread the butter between the skin and breast meat. Tie the legs with string, then lay the thyme and a bay leaf over each breast.

3 Lay the bacon over the herbs on the breasts, place the birds in the tin and season with freshly ground black pepper. Bring together the long ends of the foil, fold over securely to enclose, then seal the ends.

4 Roast the pheasants for 20 minutes, then reduce the oven temperature to 190°C/375°F/Gas 5 and cook for a further 40 minutes.

5 Uncover the birds and roast for 10–15 minutes more or until they are browned and cooked through. Transfer to a board and leave to stand, covered, for 10 minutes before carving.

6 Pour the juices from the foil into the tin and skim off any fat. Add the flour and cook, stirring, until smooth. Add the stock and redcurrant jelly and bring to the boil. Simmer the gravy until thickened, then stir in the port. Season to taste, strain and serve with the pheasants.

Main Courses

Beef Wellington

This is a luxurious and delicious way of serving a prime cut of beef.

Serves 4

INGREDIENTS
675 g/1½ lb fillet steak, tied
15 ml/1 tbsp vegetable oil
350 g/12 oz puff pastry, thawed if frozen
1 egg, beaten, to glaze
freshly ground black pepper
watercress, to garnish

FOR THE PARSLEY PANCAKES
50 g/2 oz/½ cup plain (all-purpose) flour
pinch of salt
150 ml/¼ pint/⅔ cup milk
1 egg
30 ml/2 tbsp chopped fresh parsley
a little sunflower oil, for frying

FOR THE MUSHROOM PATE
1 small onion, chopped
25 g/1 oz/2 tbsp unsalted butter
450 g/1 lb/6 cups assorted wild and
    cultivated mushrooms,
    finely chopped
75 ml/5 tbsp double (heavy) cream
50 g/2 oz/1 cup fresh white breadcrumbs
2 egg yolks

1 Preheat the oven to 220°C/425°F/Gas 7. Season the steak with pepper. On the hob, heat the oil in a roasting tin and brown the steak quickly on both sides. Transfer to the oven and roast for 15–25 minutes according to taste. Cool and remove the string. Turn the oven to 190°C/375°F/Gas 5.

2 To make the pancakes, beat the flour, salt, half the milk, the egg and parsley together until smooth, then stir in the remaining milk. Fry three or four thin pancakes in a little oil.

3 To make the pâté, fry the onion in the butter until soft. Add the mushrooms and cook until their juices evaporate. Blend in the cream, breadcrumbs and egg yolks to make a paste. Cool.

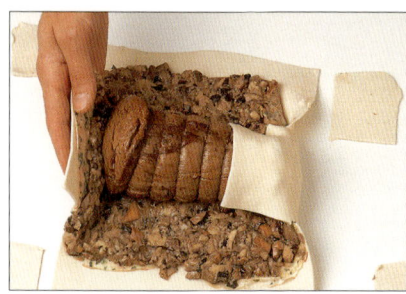

4 Roll out the pastry into a rectangle 35 x 30 cm/14 x 12 in. Place two pancakes on the pastry and spread with mushroom pâté. Place the beef on top and spread over any remaining pâté. Cover with the remaining pancakes. Cut out four squares from the corners of the pastry. Moisten the pastry edges with egg and wrap them over the meat.

5 Decorate the top with the pastry trimmings and brush with egg. Cook for 40 minutes until golden. Garnish with watercress and serve.

Venison with Cranberry Sauce

Low in fat, venison makes a healthy choice for a special occasion.

Serves 4

INGREDIENTS
1 orange
1 lemon
115 g/4 oz/1 cup fresh or
   frozen cranberries
5 ml/1 tsp grated fresh
   root ginger
1 fresh thyme sprig, plus extra
   to garnish
5 ml/1 tsp Dijon mustard
60 ml/4 tbsp redcurrant jelly
150 ml/¼ pint/⅔ cup ruby port
30 ml/2 tbsp sunflower oil
4 venison steaks
2 shallots, finely chopped
salt and freshly ground black pepper
creamy mashed potatoes and broccoli,
   to serve

1 Pare the rind from half the orange and half the lemon, leaving the pith, and cut into very fine strips. Blanch in a pan of boiling water for about 5 minutes until tender. Drain.

2 Squeeze the orange and lemon juice into a pan. Add the cranberries, ginger, thyme, mustard, redcurrant jelly and port. Cook gently until the jelly melts. Bring to the boil, cover and cook gently for 15 minutes until the berries are just tender.

3 Heat the oil in a frying pan, and fry the venison steaks over a high heat for 2–3 minutes. Turn them over and add the shallots. Cook the steaks on the other side for 2–3 minutes, depending on how well done you want them.

4 Just before the end of cooking, pour in the sauce and add the strips of citrus rind. Allow to bubble for a few seconds to thicken slightly, then remove the thyme and adjust the seasoning.

5 Serve the steaks with the sauce spooned over, garnished with thyme and accompanied by mashed potatoes and broccoli.

COOK'S TIP: When frying venison, always remember: the briefer, the better. Venison will turn to leather if subjected to fierce heat after it has reached the medium-rare stage. If you dislike any hint of pink, cook it to this stage then let it rest in a low oven for a few minutes.

Honey-roast Ham

A roast gammon joint can be a succulent addition to the Christmas table.

Serves 8–10

INGREDIENTS
2 kg/4½ lb boned gammon joint
1 onion, quartered and stuck with cloves
2 bay leaves
few black peppercorns
twist of orange peel
small piece of fresh ginger
½ cinnamon stick
few stalks of parsley

FOR THE GLAZE
cloves
90 ml/6 tbsp clear honey
30 ml/2 tbsp wholegrain mustard

1 Weigh the ham and calculate the cooking time, allowing 20 minutes per 450 g/1 lb, plus 20 minutes extra. Place the meat in a large pan and cover it carefully with cold water. Bring to the boil, then pour off the water.

2 Rinse the pan and replace the joint. Cover it with cold water and add the onion and remaining flavouring ingredients to taste.

3 Bring the water slowly to the boil, cover the pan and leave to simmer for the calculated cooking time less 15 minutes. If cooking a 2 kg/4½ lb ham this would be 1 hour 35 minutes.

4 Remove the ham joint from the pan and allow to cool slightly. Cut off the rind (zest) and score the fat in a diamond pattern. Preheat the oven to 180°C/350°F/Gas 4.

5 For the glaze, press the cloves into the fat of the ham at intervals. Mix together the honey and wholegrain mustard and spread the mixture over the fat. Wrap the ham in foil, leaving only the glazed area uncovered.

6 Place the ham, glazed-side up, in a roasting tin and bake for 15 minutes. Serve hot or cold.

COOK'S TIP: The process described in step 1 is for drawing off some of the salt used in curing the meat. If time permits, the joint can be soaked in cold water overnight instead.

MAIN COURSES

Monkfish, Salmon & Sole Mousseline

This attractive dish makes an ideal lighter alternative for a festive meal.

Serves 4

INGREDIENTS
225 g/8 oz monkfish, boned
225 g/8 oz sole fillets
2 egg whites
2.5 ml/½ tsp freshly grated nutmeg
250 ml/8 fl oz/1 cup
    double (heavy) cream
25 g/1 oz spinach
350 g/12 oz salmon fillet
salt and freshly ground
    white pepper
fresh dill, to garnish

FOR THE SAUCE
450 g/1 lb tomatoes

1 In a food processor fitted with a metal blade, chop the monkfish and sole with the egg whites until the mixture is smooth and firm. Transfer to a large bowl and place in the refrigerator to chill for 10 minutes.

2 Stir in the salt, pepper and grated nutmeg. Place the bowl over a bowl of ice. Beat in the cream, 15 ml/1 tbsp at a time, then chill for 30 minutes. The mixture should be firm enough to hold its own shape.

3 Preheat the oven to 180°C/350°F/Gas 4. Line 4 ramekins with greaseproof (waxed) paper. Blanch the spinach leaves in a pan and refresh under cold water. Cut the salmon fillet horizontally into thin slices.

4 Line the bases of the ramekins with a slice of salmon. Layer with spinach and mousseline mixture and finish with a layer of salmon. Cover with a piece of greaseproof paper with a pleat in the middle to allow for expansion. Place in a roasting tin and pour in boiling water to come halfway up the sides of the ramekins. Bake for 20 minutes.

MAIN COURSES

5 To make the sauce, grill the tomatoes until the skins are blackened. Remove the skins and process the flesh into a purée. Season well with salt and freshly ground white pepper.

6 Turn the warm mousseline out of the ramekins. Garnish with dill and serve with the tomato sauce.

COOK'S TIP: You buy the tail part of the monkfish, which consists of a central cartilage and two fillets. The dark outer skin has usually been removed. The thin membrane has to be cut off by the cook. Cut away from the flesh with a sharp knife and pull off.

Herb-stuffed Lemon Sole

Lemon sole tastes superb when served with this classic sauce, delicately flavoured with sorrel and vermouth.

Serves 4

INGREDIENTS
115 g/4 oz/½ cup butter
1 small onion, chopped
115 g/4 oz/1½ cups mushrooms, chopped
50 g/2 oz/1 cup fresh brown breadcrumbs
30 ml/2 tbsp chopped fresh lemon balm
4 skinless lemon sole fillets, halved
150 ml/¼ pint/⅔ cup milk
50 ml/2 fl oz/¼ cup dry white vermouth
10 ml/2 tsp lemon juice
2 egg yolks
handful of sorrel leaves
salt and freshly ground black pepper

1 Preheat the oven to 190°C/375°F/Gas 5. Heat 25 g/1 oz/2 tbsp of the butter in a frying pan and fry the onion and mushrooms until the onion is golden and the mushroom liquid has evaporated. Add the breadcrumbs and lemon balm and season to taste.

2 Place the pieces of sole, skinned side up, on a board and spread some of the filling on each. Roll up carefully from head to tail and pack the rolls tightly on their sides in a shallow casserole. Pour the milk over, cover and bake for 15 minutes.

3 In a pan, heat the vermouth until it has reduced by half. Pour into a heatproof bowl and set over a pan of gently simmering water. Add the lemon juice and egg yolks and whisk until fluffy.

COOK'S TIP: If you find that the sauce starts to separate, add another egg yolk and continue to whisk the mixture as before.

MAIN COURSES

4 Remove from the heat and continue to whisk while adding the remaining butter, a piece at a time, until smooth and glossy.

5 Reserving a few leaves, finely chop the sorrel and add to the sauce. Season and spoon over the fish. Serve garnished with the whole sorrel leaves.

MAIN COURSES

Filo Vegetable Pie

This stunning pie makes a delicious main course for vegetarians or an excellent accompaniment to cold sliced turkey or other meat dishes.

Serves 6–8

INGREDIENTS
165 g/5½ oz/11 tbsp butter
225 g/8 oz/2 cups leeks, sliced
225 g/8 oz/1¼ cups carrots, cubed
225 g/8 oz/3 cups mushrooms, sliced
225 g/8 oz/2 cups Brussels
  sprouts, quartered
2 garlic cloves, crushed
115 g/4 oz/½ cup cream cheese
115 g/4 oz/1 cup Roquefort or Stilton
  cheese, crumbled
150 ml/¼ pint/⅔ cup double (heavy) cream
2 eggs, beaten
225 g/8 oz cooking apples, peeled, cored and
  cut into 1 cm/½ in cubes
175 g/6 oz/1 cup cashew nuts or
  pine nuts, toasted
350 g/12 oz frozen filo pastry, defrosted
salt and freshly ground black pepper

1 Preheat the oven to 180°C/350°F/Gas 4. Heat 40 g/1½ oz/3 tbsp of the butter in a large pan and cook the leeks and carrots, covered, over a medium heat for 5 minutes. Add the mushrooms, sprouts and garlic and cook for another 2 minutes. Turn into a bowl and leave to cool.

2 Whisk the cheeses, cream, eggs and seasoning together in a bowl. Pour over the vegetables. Add the apples and cashew or pine nuts.

3 Melt the remaining butter. Grease a 23 cm/9 in loose-based springform cake tin (pan) with melted butter. Brush two-thirds of the filo pastry sheets with butter on one side, and use them to cover the base and sides of the tin completely, overlapping the pastry layers so that there are no gaps.

4 Spoon in the vegetable mixture and fold over the excess filo pastry to cover the filling.

MAIN COURSES

5 Brush the remaining filo sheets with melted butter and cut them into 2.5 cm/1 in strips. Cover the top of the pie with these strips, arranging them in a rough mound on top of the filling.

6 Bake for 35–45 minutes until golden brown all over. Allow to stand for 5 minutes, then remove the cake tin and serve the pie.

MAIN COURSES

Vegetable Gougère

An unusual vegetarian dish that is attractive and appetizing to serve as part of a celebratory Christmas feast.

Serves 4

INGREDIENTS
50 g/2 oz/4 tbsp butter
150 ml/¼ pint/⅔ cup water
65 g/2½ oz/ 9 tbsp plain (all-purpose) flour
2 eggs, beaten
1.5 ml/¼ tsp English mustard powder
50 g/2 oz/½ cup Cheddar or Gruyère cheese, cubed
15 ml/1 tbsp grated Parmesan cheese
15 ml/1 tbsp breadcrumbs, toasted
salt and freshly ground black pepper
10 ml/2 tsp chopped fresh parsley, to garnish

FOR THE FILLING
25 g/1 oz/2 tbsp butter
1 onion, sliced
1 garlic clove, crushed
225 g/8 oz/3 cups mushrooms, sliced
15 ml/1 tbsp plain (all-purpose) flour
400 g/14 oz can tomatoes
5 ml/1 tsp caster (superfine) sugar
225 g/8 oz/1¾ cups courgettes (zucchini), sliced thickly

1 Preheat the oven to 200°C/400°F/Gas 6. To make the choux pastry, melt the butter in a pan, add the water and bring to the boil. As soon as the liquid is boiling, take off the heat and beat in the flour all at once, until a smooth paste is formed. Turn the mixture into a large bowl and allow to cool slightly.

2 With an electric whisk, beat the eggs gradually into the paste until the mixture is glossy but firm. Season with salt, pepper and mustard powder. Fold in the cheese. Set aside.

3 To make the filling, melt the butter in a pan and cook the onion gently until soft. Add the garlic and sliced mushrooms and cook for 2–3 minutes. Stir in the flour and the tomatoes and their juice. Bring to the boil, stirring, to thicken. Season with salt, freshly ground black pepper and sugar to taste. Add the courgette slices.

MAIN COURSES

4 Butter a 1.2 litre/2 pint/5 cup ovenproof dish. Spoon the pastry in rough mounds around the sides and turn the filling into the centre. Sprinkle the Parmesan cheese and toasted breadcrumbs on top of the vegetable filling. Bake for 35–40 minutes until the pastry is well risen and golden brown. Garnish with chopped fresh parsley and serve immediately.

Potatoes Dauphinoise

Cooked in the oven, these are an excellent alternative to roast potatoes and are delicious with most main course meat or vegetarian dishes.

Serves 6

INGREDIENTS
1 kg/2¼ lb potatoes, sliced
900 ml/1½ pints/3¾ cups milk
pinch of freshly grated nutmeg
1 bay leaf
15–30 ml/1–2 tbsp butter, softened
2 or 3 garlic cloves, very
   finely chopped
45–60 ml/3–4 tbsp crème fraîche or
   whipping cream (optional)
salt and freshly ground
   black pepper

1 Put the sliced potatoes in a large pan and pour over the milk, adding more to cover if needed. Add salt and pepper, the freshly grated nutmeg and bay leaf. Bring the milk slowly to the boil over a medium heat and simmer for about 15 minutes until the potatoes just start to soften, but are not completely cooked, and the milk has thickened.

2 Preheat the oven to 180°C/350°F/Gas 4. Generously butter a 35 cm/14 in oval gratin dish or 2 litre/3½ pint/8¾ cup shallow baking dish and sprinkle the garlic over the base.

3 Using a slotted spoon, transfer the potatoes to the gratin or baking dish. Taste the milk and adjust the seasoning, then pour over enough milk to come just to the surface of the potatoes, but not cover them. Spoon a thin layer of crème fraîche or cream over the top, or if you prefer, add more of the thickened milk to cover.

4 Bake the potatoes for about 1 hour until the milk is absorbed and the top is a deep golden brown.

COOK'S TIP: This dish will keep hot in a low oven for an hour or so, without suffering; moisten the top with a little extra cream, if you like.

Roast Potatoes

Floury potatoes make the best crisp roast potatoes. Garlic or rosemary can be added to the oil, to flavour the potatoes during cooking.

Serves 4

INGREDIENTS
675 g/1½ lb potatoes
flour
olive oil
salt

1 Preheat the oven to 200°C/400°F/Gas 6. Peel the potatoes and, if large, cut them in half. Parboil the potatoes for 10 minutes. Drain.

2 Lightly score the surface of each of the potatoes with a fork. Roll them in the flour and tap them gently to remove any excess.

3 Heat 5 mm/¼ in olive oil in a shallow roasting tin (pan) until smoking hot. Put the potatoes in the hot oil and baste to coat them in oil. Roast for about an hour.

4 Baste and turn the potatoes twice during cooking. Drain on kitchen paper to remove excess oil and sprinkle with salt before serving.

COOK'S TIP: It is a good idea to roast the potatoes in a roasting tin (pan) fitted with a draining tray. This keeps them out of the oil but enables basting from the tin below.

Sweet-and-sour Red Cabbage

The cabbage can be cooked the day before and reheated for serving. It is a good accompaniment to goose, pork or strong-flavoured game dishes.

Serves 8

INGREDIENTS
900 g/2 lb red cabbage
30 ml/2 tbsp olive oil
2 large onions, sliced
2 large cooking apples, peeled, cored and sliced
30 ml/2 tbsp cider vinegar
30 ml/2 tbsp soft brown sugar
225 g/8 oz rindless streaky bacon (optional)
salt and freshly ground black pepper

1 Preheat the oven to 180°C/350°F/Gas 4. Shred the cabbage finely, discarding the hard core.

2 Heat the oil in a large, ovenproof casserole. Cook the onions over a gentle heat for 2 minutes.

3 Stir the cabbage, apples, vinegar, sugar and seasoning into the casserole. Cover and cook for 1 hour, or until very tender. Stir again halfway through cooking.

4 Chop the bacon, if using, and fry it gently in a pan until crisp. Stir it into the cabbage just before serving.

COOK'S TIP: The cabbage can be shredded in a food processor.

Brussels Sprouts & Chestnuts

The most traditional vegetable to serve with the Christmas bird.

Serves 8

INGREDIENTS
1 kg/2¼ lb Brussels sprouts
about 450 ml/¾ pint/scant 2 cups water or
   chicken stock
25 g/1 oz/2 tbsp butter
225 g/8 oz can chestnuts, rinsed
   and drained
salt (optional) and freshly ground
   black pepper

1 Cut a slice from the base of each Brussels sprout. Cut a cross in the base of large ones so that they cook evenly, and tear off the outer leaves.

2 Place the sprouts in a covered steamer over boiling stock or water. Cook for 6–8 minutes, according to size, until just tender.

3 Melt the butter in a frying pan, add the sprouts and chestnuts and stir them carefully over a medium heat for 2–3 minutes. Transfer to a warm serving dish, season, cover with foil and keep warm until ready to serve.

Right: Brussels Sprouts & Chestnuts (top); Caramelized Carrots & Button Onions

Caramelized Carrots & Button Onions

The flavour of the vegetables is enhanced by this cooking method.

Serves 8

INGREDIENTS
675 g/1½ lb carrots, trimmed, scraped
   and cut into thin rings
225 g/8 oz button (pearl) onions, peeled
40 g/1½ oz/3 tbsp butter
90 ml/6 tbsp chicken stock
15 ml/1 tbsp sugar
salt and freshly ground
   black pepper

1 Put the sliced carrots and peeled onions in a large pan, cover with salted water and bring to the boil over a high heat. Boil for 1 minute, then drain.

2 Return the vegetables to the pan, add the butter, chicken stock and sugar and bring to the boil over a moderate heat, stirring occasionally. Cover the pan and simmer over a low heat for about 10 minutes until the vegetables have absorbed all the liquid and are glossy and dry.

3 Season with salt and pepper to taste and transfer to a warm serving dish. Cover with foil and keep warm until ready to serve.

›
Stuffings for Poultry & Game

Stuffings add an extra dimension to your cooking. Some have become traditional partners, such as Roast Turkey with Chestnut Stuffing.

Apricot & Raisin Stuffing

Makes about 400 g/14 oz

INGREDIENTS
40 g/1½ oz/3 tbsp butter
1 large onion, sliced
115 g/4 oz/½ cup dried apricots, soaked and drained
115 g/4 oz/¾ cup seedless raisins
juice and grated rind of 1 orange
1 cooking apple, peeled, cored and chopped
115 g/4 oz/2 cups fresh white breadcrumbs
1.5 ml/¼ tsp ground ginger
salt and freshly ground black pepper

1 Heat the butter in a small pan and fry the onion over a moderate heat for about 3 minutes until it is translucent.

2 Roughly chop the apricots and put them into a bowl. Add the onions, raisins, orange juice and rind, apple, breadcrumbs and ginger.

3 Season the mixture with salt and freshly ground black pepper. Allow the stuffing to cool and use to pack the neck end of a roasting bird.

Cranberry & Rice Stuffing

Makes about 450 g/1 lb

INGREDIENTS
225 g/8 oz/generous 1 cup long grain rice, washed and drained
600 ml/1 pint/2½ cups meat or poultry stock
50 g/2 oz/4 tbsp butter
1 large onion, chopped
150 g/5 oz/1¼ cups cranberries
60 ml/4 tbsp orange juice
15 ml/1 tbsp chopped fresh parsley
10 ml/2 tsp chopped fresh thyme
freshly grated nutmeg
salt and freshly ground black pepper

1 Put the rice and stock into a small pan, bring to the boil and stir. Cover and simmer for 15 minutes until the stock has been absorbed. Tip the rice into a bowl and set aside.

2 Heat the butter in a small pan and fry the onion for about 3 minutes until it is translucent. Add it to the rice in the bowl.

3 Put the cranberries and orange juice in the cleaned pan and simmer until tender. Tip the fruit and any juice into the rice bowl. Add the herbs and season to taste with nutmeg, salt and pepper. Allow to cool and use to pack the neck end of a turkey.

Vegetables & Stuffings

Chestnut Stuffing

Makes about 400 g/14 oz

INGREDIENTS
40 g/1½ oz/3 tbsp butter
1 large onion, chopped
450 g/1 lb can unsweetened chestnut purée
50 g/2 oz/1 cup fresh white breadcrumbs
45 ml/3 tbsp orange juice
freshly grated nutmeg
2.5 ml/½ tsp caster sugar
15 ml/1 tbsp chopped fresh parsley
salt and freshly ground black pepper

1 Heat the butter in a pan and fry the onion over a moderate heat for about 3 minutes until it is translucent.

2 Remove the onion from the heat and mix it with the chestnut purée, breadcrumbs, orange juice, freshly grated nutmeg, sugar and parsley.

3 Season with salt and pepper. Allow to cool and use to pack the neck end of a turkey.

Above (clockwise, from left): Apricot & Raisin Stuffing; Chestnut Stuffing; Cranberry & Rice Stuffing

Poached Pears in Port Syrup

A richly colourful but lighter dessert option, suitable for entertaining.

Serves 4

INGREDIENTS
2 ripe, firm pears, such as Williams, or Comice
pared rind of 1 lemon
175 ml/6 fl oz/¾ cup ruby port
50 g/2 oz/¼ cup caster (superfine) sugar
1 cinnamon stick
60 ml/4 tbsp cold water
fresh cream, to serve

FOR THE DECORATION
30 ml/2 tbsp sliced
    hazelnuts, toasted
fresh mint, pear or
    rose leaves

1 Peel the pears, cut them in half and remove the cores. Place the lemon rind, port, sugar, cinnamon stick and water in a shallow pan. Bring to the boil over a low heat.

2 Add the pears, lower the heat, cover and poach for 5 minutes. Let the pears cool in the syrup.

3 When the pears are cold, transfer them to a bowl with a slotted spoon. Return the syrup to the heat. Boil rapidly until it has reduced and will lightly coat the back of a spoon. Discard the cinnamon stick and lemon rind and leave the syrup to cool.

4 To serve, place each pear half in turn on a board, cut side down. Keeping it intact at the stalk end, slice it lengthways, then, using a palette knife, carefully lift it off and place on a dessert plate. Press gently to fan out.

5 Spoon the port syrup over the pears. Top each portion with a few hazelnuts and decorate with fresh mint, pear or rose leaves. Serve with cream.

Ginger Trifle

This festive dessert is a good way to use up leftover cake, whether plain, chocolate or gingerbread. You can substitute clear honey for the ginger and syrup, if you prefer.

Serves 8

INGREDIENTS
225 g/8 oz gingerbread or other cake
60 ml/4 tbsp Grand Marnier or sweet sherry
2 ripe dessert pears, peeled, cored and cubed
2 bananas, thickly sliced
2 oranges, segmented
1–2 pieces preserved stem ginger, finely chopped, plus 30 ml/2 tbsp syrup

FOR THE CUSTARD
2 eggs
50 g/2 oz/¼ cup caster (superfine) sugar
15 ml/1 tbsp cornflour (cornstarch)
450 ml/¾ pint/scant 2 cups milk
few drops of vanilla extract

FOR THE DECORATION
150 ml/¼ pint/⅔ cup double (heavy) cream, lightly whipped
25 g/1 oz/¼ cup chopped almonds, toasted
4 glacé (candied) cherries
8 small pieces angelica

1 Cut the gingerbread or cake into 4 cm/1½ in cubes. Put them in the base of a 1.75 litre/3 pint/7½ cup glass bowl. Sprinkle over the Grand Marnier or sherry and leave to soak in.

2 To make the custard, whisk the eggs, sugar and cornflour together in a bowl with a little of the milk. Heat the remaining milk until it is almost boiling. Pour it on to the egg mixture, whisking all the time.

3 Return the custard mixture to the pan and stir over the heat until thickened. Simmer for 2 minutes to cook the cornflour. Add the vanilla essence and leave the custard to cool.

4 Mix all the prepared fruit with the finely chopped preserved stem ginger and syrup. Spoon into the bowl on top of the gingerbread or cake. Cover with custard and chill until set.

5 Cover the top with whipped cream and scatter with toasted almonds. Arrange the glacé cherries and angelica around the edge.

Christmas Pudding

The classic Christmas dessert. Wrap it in muslin and store it in an airtight container for up to a year for the flavours to develop.

Serves 8

INGREDIENTS
115 g/4 oz/1 cup plain (all-purpose) flour
pinch of salt
5 ml/1 tsp mixed (apple pie) spice
2.5 ml/½ tsp ground cinnamon
1.5 ml/¼ tsp freshly grated nutmeg
225 g/8 oz/1 cup grated suet
1 dessert apple, grated
225 g/8 oz/4 cups fresh white breadcrumbs
350 g/12 oz/1½ cups soft brown sugar
50 g/2 oz/½ cup flaked (sliced) almonds
225 g/8 oz/1½ cups seedless raisins
225 g/8 oz/1 cup currants
225 g/8 oz/1⅓ cups sultanas (golden raisins)
115 g/4 oz/½ cup ready-to-eat dried apricots
115 g/4 oz/⅔ cup chopped mixed peel
finely grated rind (zest) and juice of 1 lemon
30 ml/2 tbsp black treacle (molasses)
3 eggs
300 ml/½ pint/1¼ cups milk
30 ml/2 tbsp rum
holly, to decorate

FOR THE BRANDY BUTTER
75 g/3 oz/6 tbsp unsalted butter
75 g/3 oz/6 tbsp caster (superfine) sugar
finely grated rind (zest) of 1 small orange
45 ml/3 tbsp brandy

1 Sift the flour, salt and spices into a large bowl. Add the fat, apple and other dry ingredients, including the grated lemon rind.

2 Heat the treacle until warm and runny and pour into the dry ingredients. Mix together the eggs, milk, rum and lemon juice and stir into the dry mixture.

3 Spoon the mixture into 2 individual 1.2 litre/2 pint/5 cup basins. Overwrap the puddings with baking parchment, pleated to allow for expansion, and tie in place with string. Steam the puddings in a steamer or large pan of boiling water for 10 hours. Remove, cool and store, covered with fresh baking parchment and cloths.

DESSERTS, PUDDINGS & BAKING

4 On Christmas day, boil the puddings for 3 hours. To make the brandy butter, whisk the butter, sugar and orange rind together until soft and fluffy. Whisk in the brandy, then chill.

5 Serve the Christmas puddings piping hot, decorated with sprigs of holly and accompanied by the chilled brandy butter.

Chocolate Yule Log

This makes a delicious alternative to Christmas cake and is a real treat for chocolate lovers.

Makes 1 large log

INGREDIENTS
3 eggs
75 g/3 oz/6 tbsp caster (superfine) sugar, plus extra for sprinkling
65 g/2½ oz/ 9 tbsp self-raising (self-rising) flour
15 g/½ oz/1 tbsp unsweetened cocoa powder

FOR THE CHOCOLATE CREAM
75 g/3 oz/5 tbsp caster (superfine) sugar
75 ml/5 tbsp water
3 egg yolks
175 g/6 oz/¾ cup unsalted butter
75 g/3 oz plain (semisweet) chocolate, melted

FOR THE DECORATION
75 g/3 oz marzipan
green and red food colourings
icing (confectioners') sugar and cocoa powder, for dusting

1 Preheat the oven to 190°C/375°F/Gas 5. Grease and line a 33 x 23cm/13 x 9 in Swiss roll tin (jelly roll pan). Whisk the eggs and sugar in a heatproof bowl over a pan of simmering water until thick and pale, then remove from the pan. Continue whisking until cool and the whisk leaves a trail on the surface.

2 Gently fold in the flour and cocoa and pour the mixture into the tin. Bake for 18–20 minutes or until the cake springs back when lightly pressed in the middle.

3 Sprinkle a sheet of baking parchment with caster sugar. Invert the cake on to the paper and remove the lining paper. Trim off the edges and, starting from a short edge, carefully roll up the cake and paper.

4 To make the chocolate cream, dissolve the sugar in the water in a pan, then boil rapidly until it reaches thread stage (107°C/225°F on a sugar thermometer). Whisk the sugar syrup into the yolks in a bowl until thick and pale. Allow to cool. Beat the butter until light and fluffy then beat the egg mixture into the butter until thick. Fold in the chocolate.

DESSERTS, PUDDINGS & BAKING

5 Unroll the cake and discard the paper. Spread with half the chocolate cream and re-roll. Spread the outside with the remaining chocolate cream and mark the surface to make it look like bark. Chill to set.

6 Colour one-third of the marzipan green and a tiny piece red, with the food colourings. Decorate with holly made from the green and red marzipan and toadstools from the plain. Dust with icing sugar and cocoa.

Mince Pies

Home-made mince pies are so much nicer than shop-bought ones, especially with this unusual orange cinnamon pastry.

Makes 18

INGREDIENTS
225 g/8 oz/2 cups plain (all-purpose) flour
40 g/1½ oz/generous ¼ cup icing (confectioners') sugar
10 ml/2 tsp ground cinnamon
150 g/5 oz/⅔ cup butter
grated rind of 1 orange
about 60 ml/4 tbsp ice-cold water
1 egg beaten, to glaze
icing (confectioners') sugar, for dusting

FOR THE MINCEMEAT
150 g/5 oz/1 cup shredded suet
225 g/8 oz/1 cup currants
1 large cooking apple, coarsely grated
grated rind (zest) of 2 lemons
grated rind (zest) and juice of 1 orange
115 g/4 oz/½ cup ready-to-eat prunes, chopped
115 g/4 oz/⅔ cup stoned (pitted) dates, chopped
150 g/5 oz/1 cup raisins
225 g/8 oz/1⅓ cups sultanas (golden raisins)
115 g/4 oz/1 cup flaked (sliced) almonds
90 ml/6 tbsp clear honey
60 ml/4 tbsp brandy or rum
5 ml/1 tsp ground mixed (apple pie) spice
2.5 ml/½ tsp ground cloves

1 To make the mincemeat, mix all the ingredients together in a large bowl. Cover and store in a cool place for 2 days, stirring occasionally.

2 Sift together the flour, icing sugar and cinnamon, then rub in the butter until it forms crumbs. Stir in the grated orange rind.

3 Mix to a firm dough with the ice-cold water. Knead lightly, then roll out to a 5 mm/¼ in thickness. Using a 6 cm/2½ in round cutter, cut out 18 circles, re-rolling as necessary. Then cut out 18 smaller 5 cm/2 in circles.

4 Line two bun tins (muffin pans) with the 18 larger circles. Put a small spoonful of mincemeat into each case and top with the smaller circles, pressing the edges to seal.

5 Make a small hole in the top of each pie and glaze with egg. Place in the refrigerator for 30 minutes. Preheat the oven to 200°C/400°F/Gas 6 and bake the pies for 15–20 minutes until golden brown. Cool on wire racks. Serve warm, dusted with icing sugar.

Moist & Rich Christmas Cake

The cake can be made 4–6 weeks before Christmas. During this time, pierce the cake with a fine needle in several places and spoon over 30–45 ml/2–3 tbsp brandy.

Makes 1 cake

INGREDIENTS
225 g/8 oz/1⅓ cups sultanas (golden raisins)
225 g/8 oz/1 cup currants
225 g/8 oz/1½ cups raisins
115 g/4 oz/½ cup prunes, stoned (pitted) and chopped
50 g/2 oz/¼ cup glacé (candied) cherries, halved
50 g/2 oz/⅓ cup mixed candied citrus peel, chopped
45 ml/3 tbsp brandy or sherry
225 g/8 oz/2 cups plain (all-purpose) flour
pinch of salt
2.5 ml/½ tsp ground cinnamon
2.5 ml/½ tsp freshly grated nutmeg
15 ml/1 tbsp unsweetened cocoa powder
225 g/8 oz/1 cup butter
225 g/8 oz/1 cup dark brown sugar
4 large eggs
finely grated rind (zest) of 1 orange or lemon
50 g/2 oz/½ cup ground almonds
50 g/2 oz/½ cup chopped (sliced) almonds

FOR THE DECORATION
60 ml/4 tbsp apricot jam
25 cm/10 in round cake board
450 g/1 lb ready-made almond paste
450 g/1 lb white fondant icing
225 g/8 oz royal icing
1.5 m/1½ yds ribbon

1 Soak the dried fruit in the brandy or sherry overnight. Grease a 20 cm/8 in round cake tin (pan) and line with a double thickness of baking parchment. Preheat the oven to 160°C/325°F/Gas 3.

2 Sift together the flour, salt, spices and cocoa. Whisk the butter and sugar until fluffy and beat in the eggs. Mix in the citrus rind, the ground and chopped almonds, dried fruits (with any liquid) and the flour mixture.

3 Spoon into the tin and level the top. Bake for 3 hours, or until a fine skewer inserted into the middle comes out clean. Cool in the tin on a wire rack for 1 hour, then turn out on to the rack, but leave the paper on. When cold, wrap tightly in foil and store in a cool place. Warm, then sieve (strain) the apricot jam to make a glaze.

4 Remove the paper from the cake, place it in the centre of the cake board and brush with hot apricot glaze. Cover with a layer of almond paste and then a layer of fondant icing. Pipe a border around the base with royal icing. Tie a ribbon around the side. Decorate with holly and a bell made from the fondant icing trimmings, attached with royal icing.

Stollen

An Austrian spiced fruit bread with a marzipan filling served at Christmas.

Serves 10

INGREDIENTS
50 g/2 oz/¼ cup currants
75 g/3 oz/½ cup raisins
40 g/1½ oz/¼ cup chopped mixed peel
40 g/1½ oz/scant ¼ cup glacé (candied) cherries, rinsed, dried and quartered
30 ml/2 tbsp rum
50 g/2 oz/¼ cup butter
175 ml/6 fl oz/¾ cup milk
25 g/1 oz/2 tbsp caster (superfine) sugar
375 g/13 oz/3¼ cups strong white bread flour
1.5 ml/¼ tsp salt
2.5 ml/½ tsp ground nutmeg
2.5 ml/½ tsp ground cinnamon
seeds from 3 cardamom pods, crushed
1 sachet easy-blend (rapid rise) dried yeast
grated rind (zest) of 1 lemon
1 egg, beaten
40 g/½ oz/2 tbsp flaked (sliced) almonds
175 g/6 oz ready-made marzipan
melted butter, for brushing
icing (confectioners') sugar, for dusting

1 Soak the dried and candied fruit in the rum. Heat the butter, milk and caster sugar in a pan until the sugar has dissolved and the butter has melted. Cool until hand-hot.

2 Sift the flour, salt, nutmeg and cinnamon into a bowl and add the cardamom and yeast. Make a well and stir in the milk mixture, lemon rind and egg. Beat to form a soft dough.

3 Turn on to a floured surface. With floured hands, knead the dough for about 5 minutes. Knead in the soaked fruit and almonds. Return the dough to the clean, oiled bowl, cover with clear film and leave in a warm place for up to 3 hours until doubled in bulk.

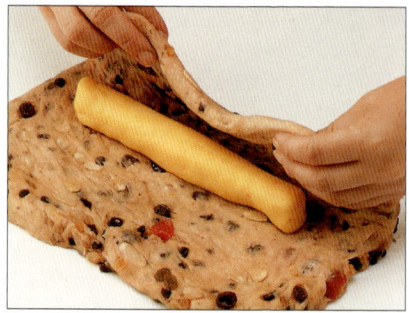

4 Knead the dough for 1–2 minutes on a floured surface, then roll out to a 25 cm/10 in square. Roll the marzipan to a slightly shorter sausage shape and place in the centre. Fold over both sides of the dough to cover the marzipan. Seal the ends.

DESSERTS, PUDDINGS & BAKING

5 Place the roll, seam side down, on greased baking parchment. Cover with oiled clear film and leave in a warm place until doubled in bulk. Preheat the oven to 190°C/375°F/Gas 5.

6 Bake for 40 minutes or until golden brown and hollow-sounding when tapped underneath. Brush the hot stollen with melted butter and dredge with icing sugar.

Index

Apples: Roast Goose with Caramelized Apples, 24-5
Apricot & Raisin Stuffing, 48-9

Beef Wellington, 28-9
Brandy Butter, 54
Broccoli & Almond Soup, 11
Brussels Sprouts & Chestnuts, 46-7

Cakes: Chocolate Yule Log, 56-7
Moist & Rich Christmas Cake, 60-1
Carrots, Caramelized, 46-7
Cheese: Roquefort & Cucumber Mousse, 16-17
Stilton Tartlets, 20-1
Chestnuts: Brussels Sprouts & Chestnuts, 46-7
Chestnut Stuffing, 49

Chicken Liver Pâté, 18-19
Chocolate Yule Log, 56-7
Christmas Pudding, 54-5
Cranberries: Cranberry & Rice Stuffing, 48-9
Cranberry Sauce, 9
Venison with Cranberry Sauce, 30-1

Filo Vegetable Pie, 38-9
Fondant Icing, 9

Ginger Trifle, 52-3
Goose, Roast with Caramelized Apples, 24-5
Gougère, Vegetable, 40-1

Ham, Honey-roast, 32-3

Icings, 9

Mince Pies, 58-9
Monkfish, Salmon & Sole Mousseline, 34-5

Onions: Caramelized, 46-7
chopping, 8

Pâté, Chicken Liver, 18-19
Pears: Pear & Watercress Soup, 10
Pears, Poached in Port Syrup, 50-1
Pheasant, Roast with Port, 26-7
Potatoes: Potatoes Dauphinoise, 42-3
Roast Potatoes, 44

Red Cabbage, Sweet-and-sour, 45
Roquefort & Cucumber Mousse, 16-17
Royal Icing, 9

Salad, Christmas, 12-13

Salmon Terrine, Layered, 14-15
Sole: Herb-stuffed Lemon Sole, 36-7
Soups, 10-11
Stilton Tartlets, 20-1
Stollen, 62-3
Stuffings, 48-9

Timetable, 6
Trifle, Ginger, 52-3
Turkey: carving, 7
Roast Turkey, 7, 22-3

Vegetables, 8, 42-6
Filo Vegetable Pie, 38-9
Vegetable Gougère, 40-1
Venison with Cranberry Sauce, 30-1

Yule Log, Chocolate, 56-7

This edition is published by Lorenz Books,
an imprint of Anness Publishing Ltd,
Blaby Road, Wigston, LE18 4SE

www.lorenzbooks.com; www.annesspublishing.com

If you like the images in this book and would like to investigate using them for publishing, promotions or advertising, please visit our website www.practicalpictures.com for more information.

Publisher: Joanna Lorenz
Editor: Valerie Ferguson & Helen Sudell
Series Designer: Bobbie Colgate Stone
Designer: Andrew Heath
Production Controller: Steve Lang

Recipes contributed by: Carole Clements, Roz Denny, Nicola Diggins, Shirley Gill, Lesley Mackley, Sue Maggs, Maggie Mayhew, Norma Miller, Janice Murfitt, Annie Nichols, Katherine Richmond, Liz Trigg, Pamela Westland, Steven Wheeler, Elizabeth Wolf-Cohen.

Photography: William Adams-Lingwood, Karl Adamson, Edward Allwright, James Duncan, John Freeman, Michelle Garrett, Nelson Hargreaves, Amanda Heywood, David Jordan, Michael Michaels.

All rights reserved. No part of this publication may be reproduced, stored in a retrieval system, or transmitted in any way or by any means, electronic, mechanical, photocopying, recording or otherwise, without the prior written permission of the copyright holder.

A CIP catalogue record for this book is available from the British Library

Cook's Notes

Bracketed terms are intended for American readers.

For all recipes, quantities are given in both metric and imperial measures and, where appropriate, in standard cups and spoons. Follow one set of measures, but not a mixture, because they are not interchangeable.

Standard spoon and cup measures are level. 1 tsp = 5ml, 1 tbsp = 15ml, 1 cup = 250ml/8fl oz. Australian standard tablespoons are 20ml. Australian readers should use 3 tsp in place of 1 tbsp for measuring small quantities.

American pints are 16fl oz/2 cups. American readers should use 20fl oz/2.5 cups in place of 1 pint when measuring liquids.

Electric oven temperatures in this book are for conventional ovens. When using a fan oven, the temperature will probably need to be reduced by about 10–20°C/20–40°F. Since ovens vary, you should check with your manufacturer's instruction book for guidance.

Medium (US large) eggs are used unless otherwise stated.

Publisher's Note:

Although the advice and information in this book are believed to be accurate and true at the time of going to press, neither the authors nor the publisher can accept any legal responsibility or liability for any errors or omissions that may have been made nor for any inaccuracies nor for any loss, harm or injury that comes about following instructions or advice in this book.

© Anness Publishing Limited 2013

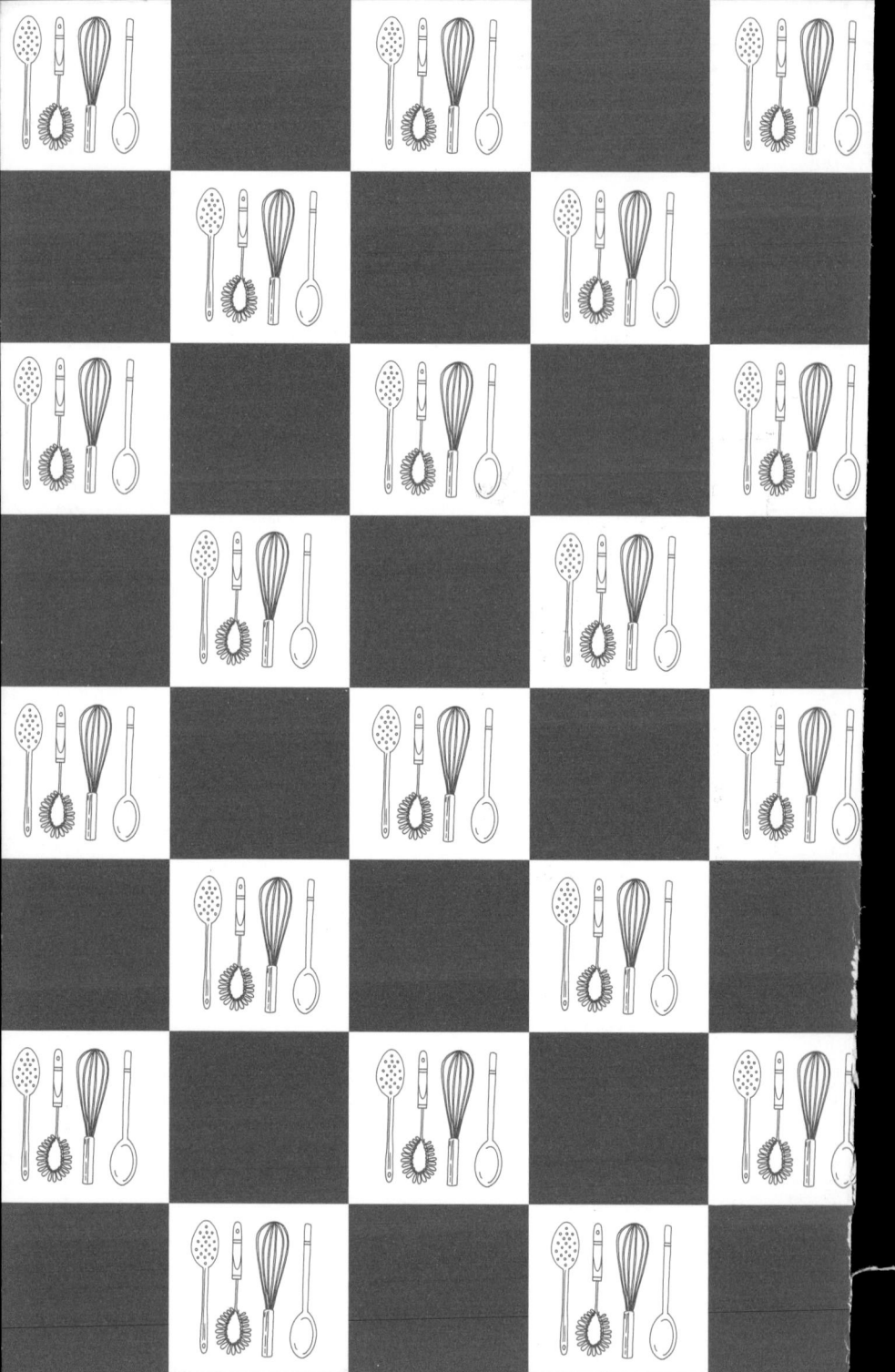